# Condor Magic

Written by Lyn Littlefield Hoopes

Paintings by Peter C. Stone

For Claude, with love and thanks
~ Lyn Littlefield Hoopes

For Amanda, Sara, and Oliver,
with love
~ Peter C. Stone

**HSUS**

The Humane Society
of the United States

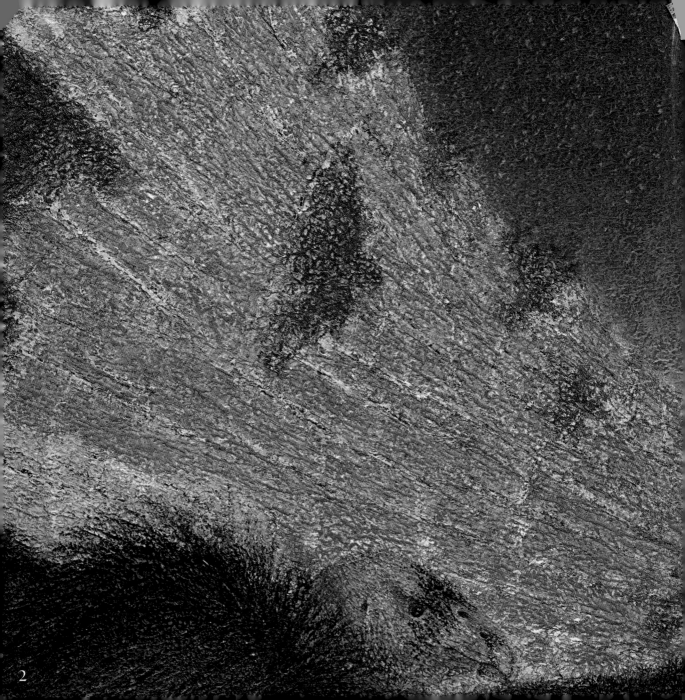

*I*magine a leap
out into the sky.
a flap of wings
and you're into the blue.
Yes, you:
you can soar!
You're the magical, wild condor.

The giant condor of California,
a rare bird, let me warn you.

As a soaring bird,
you are one of the best.
For you, it's largely effortless.
You ride the thermals,
The warm winds lift,
sweep you up,
you float and drift,
circle, spiral,
you climb quite high
on a wild, warm pocket of sky.

At the tip of your wings
are your feathers of flight
—seven primaries—
now tilt them right.
Tip them, turn them, let them guide,
guide to where you can catch a ride.
Catch a ride on a rising pocket.
Shoot up like a silent rocket!
Blast off into the blue,
yes, you!
You can soar.
You're the mysterious,
wild condor.

Now this, my friend,
is how you're dressed:
your head is naked
to avoid the mess.
(You're a scavenger, confess!)
You eat sticky innards,
and gutsy mush.
Your neck feathers bristle
like a toilet brush.
Beneath your eye
is a grizzly black brow . . .

*Abracadabra!* Presto!
       Wow!

Your wings open wide
as a soccer goal,
and drape,
a sleek, feathered,
black-coal cape:
a magician's cape
with a secret white lining,
the perfect cover
for surreptitious dining . . .
dining . . . dining.

You're a curious dude,
a ravenous raven,
disgustingly crude,
rudely behaving.
From high where you're flying,
spy the dead and dying.

Swoop . . .
                dive . . .
                        drop from the sky.

Quick! A carcass you pick:
cattle, deer, squirrels, sheep.
(Let's hope they're not just asleep!)
Tell them all to beware:
anywhere there's anything
gone or going,
you'll be there!

Forty thousand years you soared
over North America, shore to shore,
the mysterious, magical, wild condor.

You fed on mammoths
and giant sloths,
saber-toothed tigers,
until they died off.

When your food got scarce,
so did you:
your numbers grew
all too few.

Across the land,
you were no more,
except on the windy,
western shore.
Perched on cliffs
of ancient stone,
man first found you
picking on bones,
resting in redwoods,
nesting in caves,
dining on sea creatures
washed up by waves.

Native Americans sang your lore,
painted and danced for the wild condor.

But then came settlers to the west,
your open space grew less and less.

Farms and ranches
brought DDT;
you were shot for sport
and curiosity.

Tangled in high wires,
your wings were torn:
your brothers died faster
than they could be born.

Soon scientists all were
fearing you were doing
some serious disappearing.

Uproar!
Condor!
On the brink!

Would you soon
be extinct?

By nineteen eighty-five,
only nine were left,
in the wild, alive.
They had to be captured
to survive.

Nine . . . eight . . .
seven . . . six . . .
could scientists breed
condor chicks?

Five . . . four . . .
three, two, one!
Have you heard . . .
you're the last bird?

The largest bird
in the western sky:
you're the oldest bird
still to fly,
the mysterious,
magical wild condor.

15

The last wild condor of California,
it's 1987, and let me warn you:
catch that thermal,
ride the bright morning,
for things will be changing
without much warning.

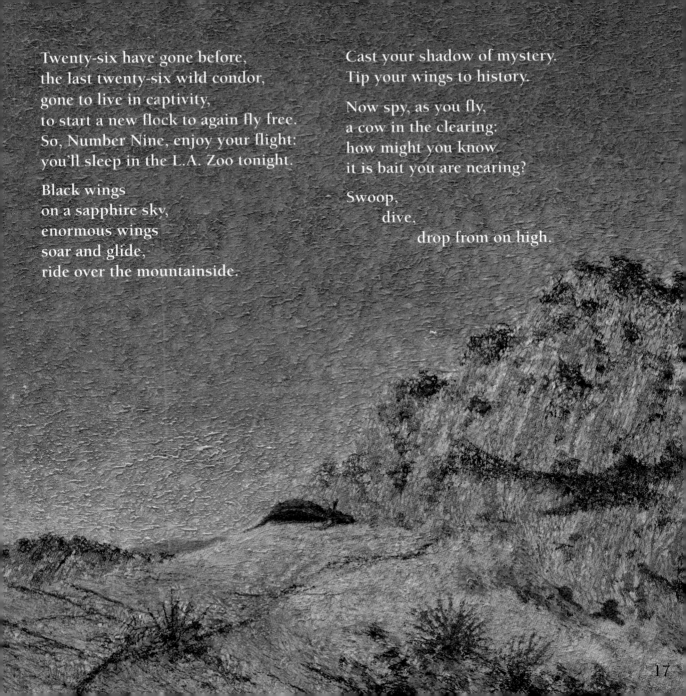

Twenty-six have gone before,
the last twenty-six wild condor,
gone to live in captivity,
to start a new flock to again fly free.
So, Number Nine, enjoy your flight:
you'll sleep in the L.A. Zoo tonight.

Black wings
on a sapphire sky,
enormous wings
soar and glide,
ride over the mountainside.

Cast your shadow of mystery.
Tip your wings to history.

Now spy, as you fly,
a cow in the clearing:
how might you know
it is bait you are nearing?

Swoop,
    dive,
        drop from on high.

17

Bounce,

    pounce,

        see the net fly.

You're the last condor
fished from the sky.

Close your great wings,
man will hold you.
Quietly, gently,
the net enfolds you.

Gather in your magician's cape.
Now one white feather
makes an escape,
slowly rises,
lifts on the wind . . .

and a new kind of magic
begins.

*I*magine an egg,
blue and speckled,
and you inside,
no bigger than a freckle.

You're a flash of sunlight,
a splash of sky;
a hint of the wild
grows in your eye.

You sleep.
You dream you fly.
You grow
talons, toes,
head wrinkled pink.
To time before time,
you're a living link.

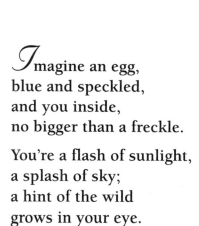

Yes, you . . .
so new,
so very old.
You hold
the story of a world untold.

You sleep.
You grow
for eight long weeks.
An egg tooth rises
on your beak.

You grow wings,
and a bold red eye.
You dream you fly,
double-dips on an open sky,
a sweeping shadow
on the canyon floor...

the mysterious,
magical,
wild condor.

*P*ip!
The first chip.
Egg tooth, strike!
Whack! Thwack!
Arch your back.
Open a crack!

Pop!
Off with the top!
Now, stretch, uncurl.
Slowly, let your wings
unfurl.

You're a chick,
all slick
in sticky egg stuff.

Soon you will dry
into downy fluff,
fluffy, silky, milky white down.
Its 1996, chick,
take a look around.

You're a condor,
yes, you.
Welcome to the zoo!

Shshshshsh!
Quietly working,
hoping, yearning,
uncovering your secrets,
scientists are learning.

They whisper
among you,
watching, waiting,
tracking condors
dating, mating,
baby condors
incubating,
fledgling birds
trying flying . . .

Have you heard?
Scientists are spying . . .
everywhere sneaking,
hiding, pecking,
stealing eggs
so mothers lay others—
more sisters,
more brothers—
feeding little chicks,
a puppet on a hand,
watching through blinds,
so you won't see man . . .

. . . won't see man.

Now, flap your wings
and touch beaks.
Mama will feed you
these early weeks,
food from the crop
where she holds her store,
scraps of gutsy carrion gore.

Beware, items may shift
in flight:
*Abracadabra!*
Take a bite!

25

*H*op!
Flap!
Hop!
Flap! Flap! Flap!

Young condors of all ages
are trying flying
in large flight cages.

Now you lose
your fluffy down.
How you grow
by leaps and bounds,
hopping and waiting
for feathers to come in,
leaping and flapping,
until flying can begin . . .

. . . flying can begin.

Do you feel the wind?

There's a knowing growing
in your bold red eye:
you see wild wings
on a sapphire sky.

Slowly, you are gaining
your great flight feathers,
skin color changing
to apricot leather.

Your wings grow grand,
a ten-foot span.
You dream of sailing
over sea and land,
soaring, circling,
swooping low,
diving to greet
your shadow below.

Listen!
Scientists are on the spy.
Who will they choose
to take to the sky—
to fly?

You!
    Yes, you!

        Welcome to the blue!

*B*lue before you
as far as you see,
blue sky to infinity.
House Rock Valley, Arizona,
a protected place
for a magical loner.

Scientists will feed you here,
watch you mornings calm and clear.
You'll race your shadow
on sandstone cliffs,
glide over valleys, ride the lifts,
dodge the eagle's swift tail-chase,
light on the redrock canyon face.

Now perched in a pen
high on the ledge,
six stand, wings tagged,
in full fledge.
A countdown echoes
from far below.
"Welcome back, brother,"
chant the Navajo,
a prayer for you
to rise and soar.

Suddenly,
    silently,
        up goes the door.

"Ten . . . nine . . . eight . . .
seven . . . six . . ."
Six young condors
out on the cliff:
five, plus you,
wait for a lift.

"Four . . . three . . . two . . . one!"
Open your wings
to the morning sun!

You're condor number thirty six . . .
*Abracadabra!*
Show us your tricks!

Imagine a leap
out into the sky . . .

Now . . .

# Fly!

Flap your wings!
You're into the blue!
Yes, You!

You can soar!